Animal Tales

Confessions of a Humane Investigator/ACO

Eugene Elander

Humanities

ACADEMIC PUBLISHERS

ISBN: 978-1-98-855749-6

Published in New Zealand

A catalogue record for this book is available from the National Library of New Zealand.

Kei te pātengi raraunga o Te Puna Mātauranga o Aotearoa te whakarārangi o tēnei pukapuka.

DEDICATION

*This book is dedicated in loving memory
of all the Companion Animals which have
shared our lives; those since 2002 are:*

DOGS:

Maja

Tucker

Domino

Wolfgang

CATS:

Stina

MorMor

AnnaBelle

Loki (in Gotland)

*May they frolic forever in the
pastures of plenty!
Eugene and Birgit Elander*

ANIMAL TALES:

Confessions of a Humane Investigator/ACO

TABLE OF CONTENTS

Note: ACO is the standard acronym for Animal Control Officer, usually (as in this instance) a sworn professional attached to many law enforcement departments.

PREFACE:
How it all began...

My family and I have always been lovers of companion animals, often called pets. I do not remember our first dog, a large Airedale named Ricky, as my parents were forced to part with Ricky shortly after I was born, because, as my father Martin put it, "Ricky seemed to think that you might be his snack food." Instead, my mother trained a series of cats to jump to the kitchen windowsill of our ground-floor Jamaica, New York apartment, luring them with food scraps, and then letting the cats move in with us - at least until the janitor learned of their unauthorized stay.

And then there were Rusty and Springer, the first two dogs that I remember; Rusty was rescued in New York and moved to Ohio with us when I was thirteen years old, remaining there into his old age, when he was relocated to a local veterinarian's boarding facility, where he lived out his life. Springer turned up in the middle of our Kettering,

Ohio residential street one Sunday; my father stopped traffic and we took him in "until his owner showed up" – staying for 17 years!

So, it was perhaps not at all surprising that, when a major fire closed the community care home which I had owned and operated in Vermont in the mid-1990s, leading me to search for a new position, I jumped at the opportunity presented by the Bennington County Humane Society's need for an Investigative Agent, to handle cases of animal neglect, abuse, and cruelty. The fact that I had no investigative credentials at that time did not deter me in the slightest, as having had several previous careers – ranging from college teaching to agency directorships to securities sales – I had learned that one should never set one's sights too low or be limited by past jobs. I had found that research into any prospective employer would work wonders during an interview, particularly when combined with a lot of sincerity and a touch of creativity. Thus, I was hired as the BCHS Investigative Agent, leading (along with other work noted below) to this present book.

After handling some four hundred animal cases for the area Humane Society, later renamed the Second Chance Animal Shelter - and serving as an original member of ADEPT, the State of Vermont ***Animals in Disasters Emergency Planning Team*** – I moved to New Hampshire as hazard mitigation consultant to the NH Office of Emergency Management, a grant-funded job. When that grant was exhausted, I was hired as Animal Control

Officer for police departments in the towns of both Brad-ford and Farmington, New Hampshire. The present book is based on true confessions from all three of those animal-related jobs, which can finally be told, since the Statute of Limitations now allows these true confessions to be shared in detail and in depth.

Your author hopes that you not only enjoy these Animal Tales, but that you also find them relevant to your own life. Companion animals help enrich our lives; they are our beloved friends and partners in adventures great and small, whose boundless trust in us humans is indeed one of the wonders of the world. **This book is therefore dedicated to all of the Companion Animals we have known and loved — they have been far more than just 'pets', rather serving as vital parts of our extended family.**

Eugene F. Elander, Long Beach, California, and Gotland, Sweden   Fall, 2020

Chapter One

A CHAI OF CRITTERS

In the Hebrew language, the letter symbolized by the English word *Chai* has two different meanings: *Chai* stands for the number *Eighteen*, and it also means *Life*. Hence, in a rather bizarre series of actions, inactions, and patterns, my family and I acquired *"A Chai of Critters"*: a total of eighteen companion animals at our then-home in Pownal, Vermont. The complex circumstances leading to such a substantial animal collection follow.

Our Chai of Critters consisted of three goats, six dogs, and nine cats. Upon reflection, there may be some further numerological significance to this exact combination of companion animals, all sequential multiples of the numeral three. That determination, however, is left to any competent mathematician who might wish to speculate on the matter. Here, our focus on animal acquisition begins with an explanation of its origination, and the attitude which led to such a large collection.

When I was offered, and accepted, the job of humane investigator for the Bennington County Humane Society, located in Shaftsbury, Vermont, my availability resulted from a major fire at the former Pownal Community Care Home (PCCH) in Pownal, Vermont, which I had owned and operated for several years until that fire occurred. Luckily, all of our residents exited in time. As to the cause of the fire: one of our residents insisted on smoking cigarettes, in an old shed behind our facility, even picking up butts in our driveway which had been left by nurses since we were a smoke-free facility. While all of our staff were convinced that this resident had caused the fire, no official determination was ever rendered, probably due to the incompetence of investigation. (Ironically, after a Vermont State Police officer said that this investigator "couldn't find his butt with both hands behind his back", I began my own study of sound investigative techniques.)

With PCCH closed, I needed to find another venture or activity to occupy my time, as well as to serve as a source of sufficient funds to close an "income gap" In the Hebrew language, the letter symbolized by the English word **Chai** has two different meanings: **Chai** stands for the number **Eighteen**, and it also means **Life**. Hence, in a rather bizarre series of actions, inactions, and patterns, my family and I acquired *"A Chai of Critters"*: a total of eighteen companion animals at our then-home in Pownal, Vermont. The complex circumstances leading to such a substantial animal collection follow.

Our Chai of Critters consisted of three goats, six dogs, and nine cats. Upon reflection, there may be some further numerological significance to this exact combination of companion animals, all sequential multiples of the numeral three. That determination, however, is left to any competent mathematician who might wish to speculate on the matter. Here, our focus on animal acquisition begins with an explanation of its origination, and the attitude which led to such a large collection.

Needing to find another venture or activity to both occupy my time and provide some additional income, it seemed to be serendipity when the area humane society advertised for an investigative agent just as I had been studying how to conduct effective investigations. In truth, it was "double serendipity", as my long-term interest in animal welfare went back to childhood, following my mother Anne's example, but had been limited to making annual donations to a host of animal causes ranging from the ASPCA to PETA, the latter advocating the ethical treatment of animals. Therefore, I did not hesitate in applying for, and then accepting, a part-time position as Animal Abuse, Neglect, & Cruelty Investigator for the Bennington County Humane Society.

At that time, my family and I already had a coterie of companion animals, including several dogs (Silkie, a greyhound saved from the Connecticut race track; Rascal, a small elderly mixed-breed; Tucker, a spirited foxhound, and Domino, a placid distinctive half rottweiler-half dalmatian mix; all rescues) and cats (Brandy, who had been with us for many years; Tosca, a Tuxedo cat; and two more.) Our unusual companion animals, however, were three goats acquired from Moose, a rather-legendary denizen of Pownal, Vermont who had a small farmstead down the road from us. We had actually acquired only two goats from Moose: Giles, a male pygmy goat (named for Giles Goat-Boy, the protagonist in the novel by John Barth) and Princess, a female companion goat to Giles, who had supposedly been neutered by former owner Moose. Imagine our surprise, then, on Thanksgiving morning, when a third goat appeared in our goat-house: a baby ram dropped by Princess, which had been fathered by Giles, and which we immediately named Pilgrim in honor of the holiday. (Pilgrim's birth was shortly followed by Giles' trip to a local farm where the visiting veterinarian finished the neutering process, much to Giles' dismay.)

Still, were the same competent mathematician previously noted to total up the above list of companion animals, their number to this point would only be eleven: three goats, four dogs, and four cats. In order to understand the emergence of the additional seven, one must understand a change in my philosophy and practice during my initial period as BCHS Investigative Agent.

As mentioned above, my original goals in first seeking, and then accepting, this new position, included supplementing our family income after a major fire closed our Pownal Community Care Home. However, as I began to cover animal abuse, neglect, and cruelty cases for BCHS, it began to seem that taking their money to help companion and farm animals (which also fell within my portfolio) was of somewhat-dubious morality. I began to wonder why, after following my mother's example and donating to animal causes during my entire adult life to that point, I should now reverse that exemplary practice and begin to "make money from distressed animals." True, the amount of money I was earning was rather minimal, particularly as my payments did not include mileage from my Pownal, Vermont home (near the Massachusetts border in Williamstown) to the site of each case. True, before officially starting as BCHS Investigative Agent, I took considerable training at my own cost. Nevertheless, I remained a bit bothered at getting paid for doing what any decent person should want to do as an absolute moral obligation: ***rescuing or helping animals in need.***

Dovetailing with these concerns was the reality that the Bennington County Humane Society was far from a "no-kill shelter"; rather, euthanization of animals in their care occurred regularly. If this unfortunate and deadly outcome faced only the old, the sick, or the otherwise-damaged ones, I could probably have accepted it as just part of the reality of animal shelters, as most of those in New England practiced euthanization. However, as illustrated by ***The Sad Saga of Suzi*** (Chapter Ten of this book), it was not unusual for young and healthy animals to suffer the same fate, were they to linger too long at the shelter. There were specific placement time limits in effect there.

Therefore, shortly after beginning service as Investigative Agent, I devised a scheme to move in the direction of resolving both sets of concerns. Upon taking in a companion animal which was unlikely to be placed in a "loving home" without more care than BCHS was likely to be willing or able to provide, I first took the animal to one of several cooperating veterinarians whom I got to agree to examine and help improve its placement chance by providing needed immediate care. The "quid pro quo" which encouraged such cooperation was that I would recommend such vets for consideration by companion and farm animal owners; the choice of vet, of course, was up to that owner, but a favorable recommendation from the Investigative Agent surely did not hurt! In return, I received reduced charges for these initial exams and any immediate care provided, often as simple as having a groomer trim fur, remove snags, and generally make the animal much more presentable, following which I would bring it to BCHS as a much-more-placeable animal, hence much less likely to face speedy euthanization. If BCHS knew of this extra step, it was ignored.

However, an unanticipated result of this particular dovetailing of monetary and care issues began to emerge: after becoming involved in trying to save a difficult-to-place companion animal, it was very hard to then see it euthanized at BCHS when that sad outcome was nearly inevitable. So, I began to go one step further: on occasion and when necessary, I would provide "respite care" until the animal could be placed. Such respite care was approved by BCHS as part of the Investigative Agent's discretionary authority, although one shelter manager shook his head and said I was "opening a Pandora's box of problems by taking on so many tough cases."

Those "tough cases" included some of the companion animals discussed in later chapters of this book, and ultimately included seven more dogs and cats, leading to our total of Chai or eighteen. As a case-in-point not covered elsewhere, consider The Bear, an aging Norwegian Elkhound just across the Vermont line whose owner had died; the family said the great dog's presence was a constant reminder of their loss, and just wanted it gone. Since they could not produce true-bred papers, the breed's rescue organization refused to take it; instead, I was asked to come to their homesite during its owner's funeral, which the entire family would attend, to take The Bear. Due to its advanced age, BCHS did not want to try to place the dog, so instead it joined our own menagerie, living out its life with us in peace and contentment. RIP to The Bear – and to all our other companion animals -- from *Eugene and Birgit Elander, Long Beach, California, Fall 2020.*

Chapter Two

A PRIMER ON REPARATIVE JUSTICE

All of us have heard the old adage that "the punishment should fit the crime." What many of us fail to realize, however, is that actual implementation of that adage is relatively rare in the U.S. By far the most frequent punishment imposed by our Criminal Courts is incarceration: locking up the convicted miscreant for some period of time, often with little connection to the severity of the offence. This debatable fairness is reinforced where juries decide upon, or even recommend, prison sentences for convicted offenders. Since jury service is pretty-much a "one off" citizen activity, jurors have little or no experience in making sensible sentencing decisions. Nor do the jurisdictions where elected or appointed judges decide on punishments necessarily improve on the fairness or consistency of the judicial process. Instead, such issues are usually swept under the judicial rug, with little or no justification. I recall one occasion, for example, when I asked the public defender in New London, Connecticut why he had provided so many "lukewarm defenses" of likely-innocent clients, and he responded, *"Well, if they hadn't done something wrong, they wouldn't be here in the first place."* **Such attitudes are the essence of injustice**.

Why, then, does society have so few options or alternatives to "locking people up" for their crimes? The obvious reason is that some people need to be removed from society for our protection; these are people who cannot or will not act constructively, safely, or sanely in relation to the rest of us, and hence society needs to be protected from them. Serial killers, serial rapists, and other violent or mentally-disturbed criminals fall into this category, and need incarceration. In particular, those who take away the liberty of others (such as kidnapers) clearly deserve to lose their own liberty, upon conviction, which has the additional benefit of preventing repetition.

But for most lesser crimes, particularly where no violence is involved, the logic of "locking people up" escapes me. Indeed, for decades there have been movements in the United States to remove so-called "victimless" crimes, such as gambling and prostitution, from criminal statutes. Why the consenting behavior of two or more consenting adults should be considered a criminal act is often hard to understand, particularly when so many governmental units now promote their own forms of gambling as revenue sources. My own paternal grandfather ran a "bookie joint" or "horse parlor" in Woodhaven, New York for many decades, allegedly paying off the cops to look the other way; was that worse, or any different, from so-called Off Track Betting? I think not.

When it comes to crimes against animals, though, a whole new set of issues emerges. Many cases of both companion and farm animal abuse are perpetrated by their owners, forcefully raising the issue of whether such animals are merely property, or are in truth sentient and feeling beings. If they fall into the former category, ownership rights originating in English common law would let owners pretty-much do whatever they please with their animals. However, as more-recent laws reinforce, if animals have feelings, and even rights, then abusing them is likely to be criminal.

These multiple, complex, and confusing issues in regard to the treatment, humane and inhumane, of companion and farm animals, led me to serious consideration about how such cases were treated in my own jurisdictions. The truth of the matter is that animal abuse, neglect, and even cruelty issues were not then taken very seriously by prosecutors in Southern Vermont at that time, except in high-profile cases with media attention. I began to understand that typical animal cases did not offer much gain to local prosecutors. Even if I did most of the "fieldwork", it was highly likely that the animal abuser would lawyer-up, and even that public sympathy would often be on the side of that abuser as an "innocent Vermonter" being pushed around by the authorities.

Further, while crimes against animals on occasion rose to the level of felonies, if the animal was tortured or died as a result of abuse, neglect, or cruelty, most were merely misdemeanors, with no significant penalty beyond a monetary fine. When I asked one prosecutor about this, he replied: "Do you have any idea how much office time and effort it takes to handle even a simple case?" It became increasingly clear to me that such "simple cases" would usually be either dismissed or plea bargained down to almost-nothing, while more complex cases (such as **Hoarders Within Our Borders** per Chapter Four here, or that of **The B's and The Birds** in Chapter Eight) often resulted in public sympathy leaning towards abusers, who might be seen as the innocent victims of overzealous humane agents, police, and local prosecutors "just looking for trouble."

Nevertheless, it fell to those same authorities -- and particularly to this humane agent as the first line of animal protection -- to do our absolute level best to prevent animal abuse, neglect, and cruelty in the first place, and to punish perpetrators as necessary to discourage the recurrence. What I needed to determine was some means of achieving these goals: that was when the idea of reparative justice came to me, so the concept will be briefly (and unofficially) explained here, with the caveat that these comments are my own, from experience, and not from any legal text.

Reparative justice, in principle, is intended (as the name implies) to repair a legal problem or situation, so as to render justice in that particular case. The intent is to make "the punishment truly fit the crime" -- even if that particular punishment is not the standard approach to that particular crime, and therefore may not have been enacted into official or statutory law. The result is that often reparative justice is "off the books" -- and therefore not sanctioned by the established legal system or its authorities, who typically view the idea with disdain and distaste. For a police or humane officer to practice reparative justice may ironically put him or her on the "other side of the law;" that is one reason why *Animal Tales* has had to wait this long to appear.

Case in point: my most frequent use of reparative justice involved animals, usually dogs, left in hot cars while their owners went shopping, visiting friends, or running errands. This practice is against the law in most jurisdictions, including Vermont -- but the limits on time and temperature vary widely, as does the degree of enforceability, unless the animal dies as a result of this abuse. During a brief-but-warm Vermont Summer, I would be called by Bennington Walmart shoppers who heard or saw a dog locked in a closed car or truck, with its windows only slightly down (to prevent the dog from exiting the vehicle.) Inside temperatures, as I knew from inserting a special thermometer probe, often rose to well over 130 degrees Fahrenheit; and the dog suffered or died.

So, why the need for reparative justice in such cases of obvious animal neglect, rising to the level of abuse? One must understand the Vermont mentality; companion animals are still often seen as merely the owner's property, and therefore the unfortunate serious injury or death is seen as a regrettable pure accident. Compounding this view is the myth that a small window opening is sufficient to keep a metal vehicle reasonably cool on even a hot day. Prosecutors would groan when I brought such a case to them, knowing how hard it would be to get a conviction, while public sympathy might well be on the side of the vehicle-and-dog owner. Indeed, there were even occasional cases of babies and young children left in hot cars and trucks while their blithe owners shopped or visited with friends or just "vegged out." While of course there was shock if the child died from heat stroke, there was also a rather "laissez faire" attitude towards such cases.

That is where, and why, my approach to reparative justice entered the picture. Take the case of the owner of a leading Manchester, Vermont factory outlet store, whose employees had reported that he brought his small dog to work every day, leaving the animal in the somewhat-shade of an old oak tree for hours on-end. The store clerks had first politely questioned this practice, being told that the animal was occasionally checked and was fine; when they persisted, they were then told to mind their own business, at which point I was called as Humane Investigator and asked to "do something." I appreciated the courage of those store staffers who were risking their jobs, as the store owner would undoubtedly know or guess who had complained, so I decided on telling him that a customer had noted the dog in the vehicle upon exiting the facility into the parking lot. (This type of "little white lie" was frequently needed to protect the innocent from the guilty.)

Upon meeting with the owner, the usual pattern occurred: first, denials of the practice, which had little credibility since the dog was in the vehicle that very day. Then, attempts at justifying the practice, such as how the dog would be lonely if left at home, was removed from the vehicle for walks, and so on. Finally, attacks on my right to investigate what was "no business of yours." I listened patiently to this tirade, and patiently explained that once a formal complaint was made, it had to be investigated under Vermont law, so I was just doing my job, not making accusations. However, upon showing the store owner my thermometer whose probe within his slightly-open vehicle window had registered over 130 degrees Fahrenheit, I disputed his version and told him he could well be prosecuted for animal abuse and cruelty (I did not tell him the likely negative outcome of such a prosecution, or that with his prominence in the Manchester, Vermont business community, sympathy might well be on his side and his defiance of law might be encouraged.)

Then, I offered the business owner the choice of reparative justice: if he preferred to avoid going to court, with its attendant negative publicity and the cost of an attorney, he could instead replace his dog in his hot vehicle during his lunch period. If he made it through a midday hour inside his vehicle, I would agree to drop the case. If not, he would have to agree to no longer bring the dog to work and leave it inside his vehicle. (I knew that his employees would confidentially report as to whether he kept his word in that instance.) The deal was struck -- and the store owner decided on an "early lunch" and immediately exited the store, gave me the dog, and sat down in his driver's seat. I looked at my watch, making a case note of the time. Seventeen minutes later, sweating profusely and red-in-the-face, the store owner left his vehicle and re-entered the store. After some deep breaths, he promised his dog would not be brought to work again. ***Case closed.***

Chapter Three

"TWO HORSES AND A MULE"

Every American State, and indeed virtually every nation, have laws governing treatment of domesticated animals. In the United States, some of these laws are antiquated, going back to the period when America was primarily a rural nation, while others sometimes seem bizarre. Of course, much the same might be said for some other statutes, laws, rules, and regulations. But when it comes to animals, including companion animals (aka pets) as well as farm animals, there are some unique issues.

Take, for example, a case in New England involving, not the usual companion animals – but rather a few farm animals which had essentially become an elderly farmer's family. This farmer inserted a clause in his Last Will and Testament that upon his own demise, his animal family were all to be euthanized, so that they did not suffer deprivation from losing him. While the old farmer's stance may seem conceited, there have been many fully-documented instances of animals which appeared to never get over the loss of a master or mistress, such as the dog which came to the local train each day for years to greet a master who had died; after that dog died, its statue was placed next to the track.

Predictably, a host of well-intended animal lovers, and many animal-rights organizations, vigorously objected to what they considered "cruel and unusual punishment" of innocent farm animals. Not only did the objections resound and rebound throughout my area, but many animal professionals such as shelter staff and lay leaders decided to file suit in the probate court, seeking to break the Will of the elderly farmer, and thus free his horses and mule to find new homes. I was among those who wrote strong support letters objecting to this "animal abuse" through needless euthanizing. Still, I decided to go a step further.

I drove to the farm where the horses and mule were being held pending outcome of the legal action, to visit and view them. My own training had included the techniques for judging health of farm animals. What I found were two horses and a mule literally "on their last legs" – they could barely stand up, were malnourished and scrawny, with various protruding bones, body sores, and infections. From reviewing the farmer's written records, I learned that his animals had been visited by several veterinarians, including a specialist, who all agreed that they were dying. The farmer had managed to keep them going, probably doing them a disservice in the process. Old age, whether in animals or in humans, is not a condition that can (or perhaps even should) be cured. The farmer's will and wish should have been respected, and the animals should indeed have been euthanized; I reversed my own stance, via another letter to the court immediately.

Perhaps ironically, meanwhile the probate court had heeded all objections, from animal lovers including professionals and agencies – none of which had actually seen the pair of horses and the mule – and had agreed to overturn that provision of the farmer's Will. The animals lives were "saved" and they went to other farms which had volunteered to care for them – different farms, so unfortunately they were separated from each other. It is highly likely that these animals were not done a favor by being "saved" for their brief remaining lifespan; and that the farmer who had owned them was doing the right thing by arranging for their euthanization: **a bitter lesson, perhaps, but still a valid one.**

It is truly said that "The Road to Hell is Paved with Good Intentions," and here is an excellent case in point, which should serve as a lesson to all well-intentioned animal "do-gooders." While we all know that aging, including our own, is inexorable and incurable, often so-called "animal rights" organizations and freelance animal activists -- and even mainstream animal protectors such as the ASPCA -- do not seem to fully comprehend the implications and effects of some of their noble stances. That problem can lead in turn to poor decisions, and even horrid unintended and inhumane outcomes, as in the case of "two horses and a mule" outlined above.

More than that, though, there is a very fundamental underlying issue: are domesticated animals property, comparable to other forms of property owned by humans -- or are they "sentient beings" with lives, feelings, and even rights? Increasingly, the latter view has been emerging from the shadows, leading, for example, to strengthened animal protection laws. Nevertheless, the issue is complex, and not fully resolved even in Western nations.

My own lesson learned from "two horses and a mule" is that there is nothing like actually seeing -- and fully investigating -- such situations involving animals. It is far too easy, and indeed too tempting, to try to go with secondhand reports about an animal situation or case, particularly when one wants to be on "the side of the angels." Sometimes, those angels' signals appear to be humane, when they are not, as in this case. Luckily, I learned that hard lesson early in my investigative work as both humane agent and animal control officer – and I have tried to apply it, even with our own aged companion animals. On occasion, though, with long-term companions, I have mistakenly shunned responsibility.

Case in point: Springer, our long-term Springer Spaniel rescued by my father outside our once-home in Kettering, Ohio, as mentioned in the Preface to this book. Springer was with us for nearly twenty years, through many moves around the East and Midwest, and finally ended up at the family home in New London, Connecticut, becoming aged and infirm in the due process of time. One Summer day, he turned up missing, and I first walked and then drove around our neighborhood, looking for Springer without success. Early that evening, the local Animal Control Officer showed up with Springer in his van.

It seems that Springer, who had not been neutered, was on the scent of a female dog, and had limped over a mile to Ocean Beach in that pursuit, when the ACO was called. That officer commented, "Perhaps Springer deserves a medal for his initiative and effort, but to you as his owner I must issue a citation for allowing him to stray." (Shortly afterward, Springer had to be euthanized due to severe old age – but at least he had his "final fling.")

Chapter Four

HOARDERS WITHIN OUR BORDERS

Before beginning active duty, first as a Humane Investigator in Vermont, and then as an Animal Control Officer in New Hampshire, I was required to undertake and complete extensive training in many relevant areas: following the basics of animal care and recognition of various medical and behavioral conditions (including the behavior or misbehavior of owners of companion and farm animals), I was trained in the basics of investigative techniques, animal laws, evidentiary rules, basic court procedure, and related topics. Much of this very-worthwhile training, which continued during my tenure in both types of positions, was at my own expense, since animal shelters and local police departments both have very limited training budgets in New England.

An area of growing concern presented at many such programs was the increase in the practice of animal hoarding, of which I had not been much aware prior to becoming active in handling such problems. While there were occasional stories on television news programs and in newspapers about large numbers of undernourished, ill, or even dying animals rescued from their quarters, other comparable or worse cases were handled privately by responsible agencies and hushed up. One of the reasons for this limited coverage is the avoidance of encouraging such practices.

There are wide differences among animal hoarders, including the types, breeds, and numbers of animals hoarded; the locations at which they are hoarded; the reasons for the hoarding, and the nature of those who participate in such practices. For example, animal hoarders may or may not specialize in one particular breed or type of animal, may keep them at home or off in the woods, and may be of any age, background, and demographic group. Nevertheless, there are also usual or common factors in hoarding, the most basic being that <u>the hoarder has far too many animals to be willing or able to give them necessary and proper care, causing considerable animal suffering.</u>

We have all read and seen stories of the "cat lady" or equivalent, who has dozens of scrawny and sick felines all over her very-messy home, ranging and reproducing freely, not receiving needed vaccinations and veterinary care, and often not receiving needed food and water either. Often, the media portray such hoarders as "do-gooders who are just saving excess animals from being put down." Merely having a large number of companion or farm animals does not constitute animal hoarding; particularly with farm animals, there is often a minimum number required for the farm in question to be economically viable. ***What distinguishes animal hoarding is the very poor conditions under which animals are being kept, and the poor condition of those animals.***

The psychological and social needs met by animal hoarding go beyond the issues discussed here, where our concern focuses on the practice itself, and on its consequences for all parties involved. One must note, however, that news and feature media often appear to take the side of the hoarder in such cases, who is portrayed as an innocent, and even noble, animal keeper who saves animals which would otherwise be running around loose -- or in even worse conditions than those where they were found to be living. Such news coverage discourages effective action against hoarding, even when the animals hoarded are kept under most deplorable – as well as illegal – conditions.

As a case in point, consider my very first animal hoarding complaint, which may have lacked some of the typical features of such cases, but made up for it with some unique elements. My humane society received an anonymous phone call from a North Bennington neighbor of a well-known local hunter and trapper (two very popular activities in Vermont) who was reported to be keeping more than a dozen small beagles chained to a large oak tree in his front yard, constantly and in all kinds of

December winter weather. The continual howling of the pack disturbed the neighbors' sleep at night, and the sight of so many dogs tangled by a heavy chain was offensive.

It was up to me, as the Humane Investigator, to determine if this was also a violation of law due to animal abuse, neglect, or cruelty, so I traveled to the site without giving advance notice to the owner of the beagles, in order to view and take photos of the situation, and record the dogs' loud baying. All such evidence, and my interview with their owner, could be used in any prosecution.

Upon arriving at the scene, I found the report to be accurate; fourteen beagles were tangled in a heavy locked chain around a large oak tree, barking and baying continually in sub-freezing cold, ice, and snow. When I knocked on the owner's door, wearing my official uniform, he came at once and invited me inside, commenting on how cold it was. That leading remark encouraged me, after identifying myself, to ask at once if it were not just as cold for his fourteen beagles. He replied that these were hunting dogs which needed to be "toughened up for hunting by getting used to the outdoors", further claiming that his family had engaged in such practices for years.

We then had some discussion of why so many beagles were needed for hunting, at which point I began to suspect that the beagles' owner was also an animal hoarder, as he stated that some of his beagles were "rescues from here and there" but would not identify the sources specifically. My own training had included signs of hoarding, one of which was the hoarder's reluctance to specify how his animals had been obtained, for many reasons, including possibly confiscating animals owned by others, or allowing inbreeding of his own pack, or engaging in some other dubious practice. Further, while his dogs were well-groomed, several seemed undernourished.

On the other hand, one of the major solutions for animal hoarding, i.e. confiscating the animals and turning them over to some competent humane society or breed agency for evaluation and care, did not seem to be justified at this point in this case. Nor did I foresee any enthusiasm on the part of local prosecutors to try the case in court on grounds of animal abuse, neglect, or even cruelty. The owner's family were well-known in the area, and generally well-respected; public sympathy might well be on their side, partly due to Vermonters' well-known distrust of the legal process, which was often termed "letting the government stick its nose where it doesn't belong."

I also thought of a reparative justice approach to the matter, involving chaining the dogs' owner to the same tree along with his pack, to see how much he liked being tied outside in that same bitter winter weather without any shelter, but of course that would have been illegal. So, instead, I focused on the issue of the continuous baying and barking of the dog pack, which was limited in Vermont under common law doctrine that each person is fully entitled to "quiet enjoyment of his or her home" without excessive noise or other disturbances. Once the multi-beagles' owner understood that this "quiet enjoy-ment doctrine" trumped his "hunt hardening" argument, he kept the dogs outside for only daytime periods, even building a large shelter for them. ***Case closed.***

Chapter Five

FERAL CAT MOUNTAIN

Feral cats pose special and difficult problems to both humane agents and animal control workers. A feral cat is essentially a wild animal, because even though cats in general are domesticated, not all individual felines meet that criterion. There are various reasons for this situation: sometimes, cat owners will leave unwanted kittens, and on occasion the mother cat, out in the woods, where their survival is a matter of fate and luck; the kittens then become feral, and the mother may also. Some cats live in the wild, having been born there, and are inherently feral. And some abused or neglected cats manage to escape into the wild, turning feral in order to survive.

For this particular humane agent, the usual approach to handling feral cats became increasingly unacceptable. Since such cats usually cannot be tamed successfully or "civilized", and cannot be placed in homes while they remain feral, animal shelters tend to automatically euthanize them. If I was tasked by the Bennington County Humane Society to use a humane trap to catch a feral cat, I knew that once it was taken to their Shaftsbury shelter, it would immediately be put down.

After a few months on the job, I began to feel like the Lord High Executioner of innocent feral cats. Even the humane trapping process became increasingly unpleasant, as the cat snarled and tried to bite me when I came back to the baited trap left near where it had been seen, to retrieve it. As I continued to ponder this situation, I went to a missing dog case near Sandgate, Vermont; a few words about Sandgate are in order here. There is only one road into the small town, and no roads out; the general store sells T-shirts reading, *SANDGATE: THIS ISN'T THE END OF THE WORLD, BUT YOU CAN SEE IT FROM HERE.* This town rests on the slope of a mountain, too.

I was unable to find the dog missing near Sandgate, but I did find the germ of an idea as to how to save feral cats without informing BCHS, which was likely to reject my solution as improper. While searching unsuccessfully for the lost dog, I encountered two high hills several miles apart. There were signs of rabbits and other small animals on both forested hills, but no missing dog. As I drove home from Sandgate, I began to think about placing male feral cats on one of the two hills, and female feral cats on the other one, so that both sexes would have a chance to survive --but were far enough apart to be unlikely to breed together, creating even more feral cats. I do not claim any definitive proof of the latter assertion, but I thought this was worth a try, as otherwise the feral cat would definitely be euthanized as unplaceable.

So, on my next feral cat case, I trapped a hungry female feral cat in the humane trap I always carried in my vehicle. Then, instead of driving the trap to BCHS, where the feral cat would be carefully removed by gloved technicians and then euthanized, I drove to the Sandgate area and opened the cage. The black-and-white female feral cat exited at once, glancing back at me as if to say, Thank You. I whispered, "You're on your own, kitty – Good Luck!" and went home, feeling that I had done a good deed. But, as the saying goes, "not so fast" – there is more to tell.

I averaged about one feral cat case a month, managing to trap about half of the animals reported to BCHS as falling into that category. Sometimes, it turned out that the cat was actually owned by a local person, but had gotten lost or perhaps even been taken by an unknown party and then escaped its new captivity. On one occasion, the animal involved turned out to not be a cat at all. I was called by employees at the Pottery Barn outlet store in Manchester because customers had repeatedly reported a "large striped cat" roaming woods behind the store, seemingly "homeless." At least, that was the story provided to BCHS; upon taking my humane trap to the store, baiting and setting it, I asked the staff to call me as soon as the cat was in the trap. The next day, I was called when the store opened, as an animal was indeed in the trap. Upon arriving at the scene, though, I noted a wide white stripe on the back of the so-called "cat", as well as narrow facial features of a large skunk. Using a long stick to avoid being sprayed, I managed to open the trap and release its occupant, following which Pottery Barn staff were lectured on filing false reports.

Returning to actual feral feline cases, though, my next such case involved a large male tiger cat. Having already mapped out my relocation plan, I took the feral cat to the other side of the small mountain where I had previously taken the feral female cat, rather than bringing her into BCHS to be euthanized. The specific advantage of this particular mountain is that there was a chasm between the two crests, probably the result of seismic activity in the distant past, which would stop travel from one side to the other, and also prevent the mingling of the two sexes of feral felines. There were some limitations on that desirable separation, though. In one later case, the trapped feline was pregnant, and I foresaw inbreeding of her kittens once they grew up – but I still took her to what I had come to call Feral Cat Mountain, as the lesser of the evils facing her.

Meanwhile, my failure to bring in feral cats to my humane society, for inevitable euthanization, was being noted at BCHS. That notice led first to "fogging" behavior on my part; I became dense when questioned as to why there were few if any feral cats being brought to BCHS, giving vague and unclear answers which included occasional escapes by the feral feline after it was trapped. I then found a local cat-fancier who agreed to raise the less-feral of my feral cats and "tame" them.

Since such cases were only occasional, and as mentioned previously many failed to trap the cat, I was able to populate Feral Cat Mountain during my tenure as BCHS Humane Agent. Sometimes now, years later, I speculate on the entire process, in view of the historic importance of cats in some ancient societies, such as the Egyptians and other who considered them to be sacred. Has Feral Cat Mountain turned into Feral Cat Nation, ruled by its denizens as a feline society? Are the descendants of my rescued feral cats now ruling their roost, and will they someday soon declare their independence of human-controlled Vermont and the United States of America? In that event, will this Humane Agent be viewed as the founder of their Nation, or even revered as its progenitor? As global climate change continues to move Vermont towards more-temperate climate and weather, will the descendants of my feral cat cases prosper and populate further? Will Feral Cat Mountain become a blessing or a curse; which outcome did I create through well-intended, but perhaps unwise, efforts to save these feral felines? **Only time can and will tell.**

Chapter Six

THE SMARTEST DOG IN BENNINGTON, VERMONT

During my years as Humane Investigator for the Bennington County Humane Society, I was not much concerned with the intelligence level of the animals I was helping, or for that matter, with the intelligence level of their owners or others involved in my four hundred-plus cases. Indeed, on occasion I was unsure which group had higher intelligence, as on the whole dealing with the animals was more productive, or at least satisfying, than dealing with their owners. Still, there is no doubt in my mind which case involved The Smartest Dog in Bennington, Vermont -- not only on the facts of the matter, but because the owner of that small Jack Russell Terrier told me so!

On a bright Spring day, BCHS received an anonymous call from a neighbor of the owner of The Smartest

Dog in Bennington, Vermont, who asserted that said owner would frequently get drunk and then punish his small Jack Russell Terrier by kicking it around, sometimes repeatedly, while cursing his lot in life. I held off going to the case site until late afternoon, the reported typical "kicking time," hoping to catch the owner in the act, but found all parties inside their house. Upon knocking on his door, the owner, an aging Vermonter with unkempt hair and beard, came to the door carrying a twelve-ounce glass of whisky in one hand, and a Colt pistol in the other. This did not seem an encouraging start towards resolving the dog-kicking case, but I proceeded to explain the complaint, and my need to examine his dog's condition for any bruises or other signs of abuse (including the dog's behavior upon being examined, often a telling sign of issues.)

I must admit to serious trepidation as I explained these matters, as while I had met few nasty animals in my humane investigations, the same was not true of all animal owners. Visits from any authorities are not welcome in Vermont, a State which still remembers that it was once a Republic, until incursions from Massachusetts and New York caused Vermont to join the newly formed American union in 1791. Republic of Vermont T-shirts remain quite popular, as does dislike of authority, even when it arises from Vermont law itself, as was the case with my work.

In this particular case, the presence of the large whisky tumbler in one hand and the pistol in the other hand of the dog owner caused more concern than usual, as had the case information that he was frequently drunk. Proceeding with extreme politeness, then, I put the burden of examining his Jack Russell Terrier on my employer, the Bennington County Humane Society, explaining that I was merely the "middleman acting on BCHS orders." So, I was pleasantly surprised, and greatly reassured, when the owner cordially invited me into his home, to answer all my questions and examine his dog. He even offered me a large glass of his favorite whisky, which I politely declined as being inappropriate while I was on duty. (He did not offer me another pistol, but had he done so, I would also have declined that offer, as I have never needed a weapon on the job.)

The small Jack Russell Terrier was quite friendly, allowing me to surreptitiously check for any bruises or other signs of abuse while I was petting the dog; I found a couple of sensitive spots as the dog winced when these were touched, making me more suspicious as to the owner's actions.

Meanwhile, though, the owner commented as follows: "So some nosy neighbor reported me as kicking my dog? Well, that is a bald-faced lie! And, I can prove it!" At that point, he called the dog over, and I observed that it came willingly and without having to be coerced, a good sign. The owner then said, "One!" and the dog barked once; the owner continued with "Two, Three, Four, Five!" sequentially, and the dog barked the correct number of times for each command. It was clear that this small Jack Russell Terrier was indeed smart, and perhaps even able to count higher than its owner, at least after he had been drinking several large glasses of whisky.

After this impressive demonstration, the owner turned to me, asking: "Now, does that sound like a kicked or abused dog?" My response was: "Well, that sounds like a very smart dog, probably the smartest dog in Bennington – but it has nothing to do with issues of kicking or other abuse!" I then reiterated my need, under law, to examine the dog thoroughly, which I proceeded to do. As I had noted previously, there were several sensitive spots on its flanks, which I pointed out to the owner, along with that anonymous report BCHS had received. After explaining Vermont law against animal abuse, neglect, and cruelty, and the potential penalties punishing such behavior, I notified the owner that I would return in a month to review the dog's condition at that later date.

Upon doing so, I found no further signs of kicking, nor of any other form of abuse. The owner remained cordial, this time without the whisky or the pistol, telling me he was now teaching his small Jack Russell Terrier to count up to ten. I never learned if he was successful in that goal; but, to this very day, I recall fondly The Smartest Dog in Bennington, Vermont. **Case closed.**

Chapter Seven

A LITANY OF LOST LIVER

ince this case focuses on some unfortunate actions of the Shaftsbury unit of the Vermont State Police, its narration starts with some background on the relationship between the State Police and the Bennington County Humane Society, and particularly with this Humane Investigator. In my efforts to prevent, or if necessary to punish, animal abuse, neglect, and cruelty, I worked closely with all area police and fire departments, sheriffs, constables (per Chapter Eleven of this book), and of course with the Vermont State Police, particularly with their Shaftsbury barracks near us.

While I was able to maintain cordial relationships with many individual State Troopers, barracks command officers were not particularly concerned about animal abuse, neglect, or cruelty, nor very supportive of efforts to prevent or punish violations of relevant animal protection laws. I recall some groans when intentional cruelty to animals, leading to their deaths, became a felony. On the other hand, my work as Humane Investigator freed up some Vermont State Police time to handle "serious problems" like drug usage, spousal abuse, and jacklighting deer (night hunting.)

Compounding my problem with area State Police was their botched investigation of the major fire which closed my former Pownal Community Care Home, mentioned in the Preface of this book. Even after telling the investigative officer exactly who had started the fire – a resident who insisted on smoking found cigarette butts in the barn adjacent to the Care Home, where the fire clearly started – its cause was found to be "indeterminate" by this investigator. When I asked a long-term community leader about that result, his comment was: "Your investigator couldn't find his butt with both hands behind his back!" It seemed my case was far from the only such disappointment; we were damaged as our insurance coverage would have doubled with arson.

One area of ongoing concern between the Vermont State Police Shaftsbury Unit and Humane Investigation for the Bennington County Humane Society involved the handling, or more likely mishandling, of evidence brought to the State Police evidence locker for safekeeping. For those unfamiliar with general evidentiary rules, a clear chain of evidence safekeeping and management is an absolute requirement in case handling and prosecutions; many cases are dismissed in court because of violations of chain of evidence requirements through careless, sloppy, or incompetent mishandling. During my tenure as BCHS Humane Agent, I encountered endless evidence issues.

Take, for example, the Lost Liver from the Vermont State Police locker in Shaftsbury, resulting in dismissal of a severe **cruelty to animals** case, along with criticism from the presiding judge. The case was first brought to my attention when the owner of a mixed-breed hound complained after a competent veterinarian had to euthanize his dog because it had been fatally poisoned. The dog's owner claimed that his rural land, just off the major highway between Bennington and Brattleboro, was a frequent "shortcut" used by a snowmobile club during the winter months. He had objected to this unauthorized use of his land as representing trespassing, and there had been some harsh words between the land owner and leaders of the snowmobile club, after which he had posted NO TRESPASSING signs prominently along the fence often crossed by the club.

It was the loud barking of his hound which signaled those incursions onto his land, so during the heated discussion between the land owner and the club leaders, threats had been made against the dog. Then, one winter early morning, the hound did not come for its regular meal, causing its owner to begin to search his land. He found the dog unable to move and throwing up, near the fence still often crossed by the snowmobilers, whose wires had been cut to allow such passage. Upon being taken to its nearby regular veterinarian, a poisoning diagnosis was made, followed by euthanization, as the suffering hound could not be saved. The owner wanted justice; so did I.

Upon going to the site of the poisoning later that same day, and thoroughly examining the land, I found some scraps of liver which had been gnawed by an animal. My conclusion was that this liver needed to be tested for poison, as the hound's veterinarian had determined what poison was used; and if there was a match, the case for animal abuse and cruelty would be much stronger. I carefully collected the liver scraps, put them in an official evidence bag with the date, time, and location duly noted, and transported that evidence to the Shaftsbury Vermont State Police unit.

Since state troopers did not usually linger in that facility, there was a rather-bizarre system for reaching them, involving a microphone outside the barracks which actually sent a signal to their Rutland, Vermont headquarters nearly fifty miles away. Rutland would then respond via a speaker set into the barracks wall, asking about the problem or situation; then, a state trooper would be dispatched or diverted if it was determined that such intervention was warranted. I followed this procedure, and after a half hour a cruiser pulled into the State Police parking lot and a young trooper admitted me into the barracks, where I presented the suspicious liver in the official evidence bag and was handed the necessary receipt; the liver was placed into a freezer used for perishable evidence; and **that was that**, until the case was presented to the prosecutors.

Except, it turned out **"that wasn't quite that"** when I went back to the Shaftsbury State Police barracks to retrieve my evidence, so that it could be properly tested for the suspected poison. After again going through the summoning process, using the microphone and speaker outside the barracks to summon a trooper via the Rutland headquarters, we could not find the liver sample anywhere in the evidence freezer. The trooper who responded even joked that "perhaps the guys were hungry and ate your evidence" – considering that a fatal poisoning was involved, I did not find this comment at all humorous. After exploring several possible explanations for the "lost liver," none of which turned out to be valid or even sensible, I had to report to the prosecutors that my evidence had disappeared from its locker, and it was concluded that we therefore had no solid case against the snowmobile club leaders or members. When the case was withdrawn, and the reason given, the presiding judge lectured me about rules of evidence, which seemed unfair.

No blame was placed on the Vermont State Police, in this case or several others which had had very sloppy handling, or even mishandling. For example, when I had been operating the Pownal Community Care Home, we took in some "troubled people" via the Bennington Probation Staff. One of these miscreants attacked another resident, and then told the State Police that she was the actual attacker, showing the officer some scratches on his back as "proof." I pointed out that the elderly woman accused of the attack had her fingernails filed down to flesh level, so could not possibly leave nail scratches; obviously, the actual attacker, a young male, had scratched his own back. Nevertheless, charges were filed against the elderly victim, another miscarriage of justice.

Chapter Eight

THE B'S AND THE BIRDS

ost humane investigations fall into a specific category, often one defined by law. Indeed, the three general types of humane cases named in Vermont law are **animal abuse, neglect, and cruelty to animals.** On occasion, though, a humane case is so weird, bizarre, or strange that it defies categorization. Sometimes such investigations are also very unpleasant -- but they are at least quite interesting. Here is one such humane case which occurred in Bennington, Vermont; the name of the abusers has therefore been changed to The Bennington's, or to The B's for short.

The B's admittedly detested cats, a point they made clear in newspaper interviews with the local Bennington Banner, and later made clear in district court where they were prosecuted. They felt cats were put on the planet to annoy people, defecate and breed wherever they chose, and worst-of-all, to torture and kill small birds. They also disliked cat owners as facilitators of such acts.

Based on my own investigation, along with newspaper stories and finally action in the courts, the B's therefore engaged in the practice of spray painting local owned cats. This was discovered when cat owners found their felines fur suddenly appearing in various and psychedelic colors. At that point, I was called in (along with the Bennington Police Department) to investigate what was happening, and put a stop to this animal abuse, because spray paint is a harmful chemical which can be absorbed through a cat's fur and skin, leading to serious external and internal injuries.

I began a series of early-morning visits to the neighborhood where the painted cats were found, on the north side of Bennington, as that was the time when they returned to their owners in this decorated condition. When I did not immediately catch anyone perpetrating the cat painting, I drew "abuse maps" which outlined the various street sites where such cats had been found, to see if a pattern emerged. It turned out that the spraying seemed to center on a particular large house on a heavily-wooded lot, after which I parked a few blocks away and walked to that site with my binoculars and camera, setting up temporary camp in the woods surrounding the house. It should be noted that while the land was posted NO TRESPASSING, a popular sign in Vermont, humane investigators and other police officers are specifically exempted in conducting investigations.

On the third morning of my visitation, watching the back door of the large house, an elderly woman emerged with – sure enough – a can of fluorescent spray paint which she aimed at a visiting cat, proceeding to add additional and colorful stripes to those natural ones on the cat. Upon walking around to the front mailbox, I saw that the name Bennington was noted on it, along with the house number. That information was sufficient for me to file a case report with the Bennington County Humane Society, following which I was tasked to refer the case to the district court. Since case filings are public record in Vermont, the Bennington Banner newspaper became aware of the matter; since that local paper had previously received complaints from some sprayed-cat owners, the Banner then contacted me for comments. After telling the Banner that the case was under active investigation, I decided to immediately interview the B's, before a reporter could alert them and thus muddy the waters by allowing the B's time to make up a story.

Around mid-morning that same day, then, I went to the B's house and was met by both of them. After explaining the many complaints received by BCHS, leading to my perusal of the property, I showed them copies of the recent photos I had taken. Surprisingly, far from denying that they had been spray painting local owned cats, both B's boasted of doing so "to protect the birds" and then expanded upon their love of all sorts of local birds which, they claimed, were turned into cat food after first being teased and tortured by those same local cats. It was clear that the B's saw themselves as Saviors of the Birds, and were proud of playing that role.

I could see, from the content and tone of the interview, that a lecture on "nature's way" and that the cats were merely doing what cats have done for millennia was not going to convince them to leave the cats in peace and stop spray-painting them. The B's were self-righteous and proud of their animal-abuse, even boasting that if they could have caught cats, they would have done even more. Luckily for the cats, then, both B's were well into old age and not very fast on their feet.

Later that same day, the B's were interviewed by the Bennington Banner, making their case to that newspaper. Public sympathy was quite mixed, as several sprayed-cat owners were also interviewed, who claimed their cats had never bothered any birds and were mainly house cats. It was clear from the B's own statements that they were happily prepared to spray-paint any cat which came into their range, without any requirement that this particular cat was bothering birds. Actually, "being a feline" was sufficiently offensive to lead to abuse of these cats by the B's.

By the time the case of The B's and The Birds came to court, several months later, the story had been picked up by several news services, and circulated far beyond the borders of Bennington. This made it the exception to most animal abuse, neglect, and even cruelty cases, in that now the local prosecutors saw considerable value in taking it seriously and pursuing it to the fullest extent of the law. At the same time, public opinion remained quite mixed, with cat lovers on one side, seeking justice for their favorite animals; and bird lovers on the other side, seeking fair treatment for their preferred creatures. Compounding those issues was the advanced age of the B's and the suspicion that they might not be "all there" when it came to the spray painting; therefore, as the investigative agent who initially interviewed them, I was summoned into court to give testimony.

After being sworn in, I was asked to describe the entire history of my involvement with this case, which I proceeded to do, taking nearly a half hour. My photos of Mrs. B spraying a local cat had already been entered into evidence. After listening to my testimony, the B's had their attorney ask for a "time out" so that they could meet privately with him. When the court reconvened, they changed their plea to "guilty with an explanation" and both of them explained that they were just trying to protect neighborhood birds from being stalked and attacked by those same felines. It became clearer and clearer that, indeed, the B's were not fully competent to make such decisions, and that they were not only elderly but also infirm. Therefore, in a rare case of reparative justice consistent with Chapter Two of this book, the judge gave them an optional sentence: if the B's would commit to no further spray painting or other abuse of local felines, and further would send written apologies to all local cat owners whose animals might have been sprayed (I would provide the list, based on my investigation) there would be no further sentence, no fine, no jail time or other punishment. This option had obviously been previously discussed with the B's attorney, as they immediately accepted it, and the matter was settled. **Case closed.**

Chapter Nine

OF BLACK CATS AND HALLOWEEN

While the immediate previous case had a somewhat-happy ending, that does not always occur in either humane investigations or animal control work. Contrast, for example, the present case, which deals with some special problems relating to black cats around the Halloween holiday.

As we all know, there have been superstitions involving black cat for centuries, in many lands and cultures. While cats in general are considered generally-pleasant, if independent, animals, those which happen to be all-black or nearly-all-black have been considered to cause bad luck. Of course, there are also beliefs that the bad luck can be prevented or ameliorated if upon seeing a black cat some words are said; in Sweden, for example, people make a spitting sound like *Tzvi, Tzvi, Tzvi -- Do Not Bother Me*. In America and elsewhere, folks may cross the street to avoid a black cat, or even swerve their vehicle on a roadway if such a cat is likely to cross their path. In some cult rituals, black cats are mistreated or even killed. In order to reduce such abuse, it was BCHS policy to not adopt out black cats during October, just before the Halloween holiday.

Still, cultists or others sometimes manage to misuse black cats. My worst such case occurred at a farmstead in Shaftsbury, Vermont, when I was tasked to investigate a bizarre case of feline abuse one Halloween. It is not uncommon in Vermont for people from Boston or even from New York to own summer homes in the State, which they visit occasionally at other seasons such as for skiing in the winter, or "leaf peeping" in autumn. A couple of New York TV news anchors owned this particular property, so when I received the call to see an animal abuse case on their property, I recognized their names. However, by the time I got to the site, they had left to return to New York, as their Halloween Holiday was irrevocably spoiled by what they had found on their property. Knowing the rules of evidence, the news anchors did not disturb the site.

On a field just inside their fence, thirteen all-black shorthaired cats had been strangled and then placed in a complete circle, heads inside so that they all faced each other. The crime was quite recent, as indicated from the cats bodily condition. After taking a complete set of photos, I called an area veterinarian for a crime scene analysis, and also contacted the Vermont State Police since this case rose to the level of a felony under Vermont law. At some point, the cats were removed from the property, but I was not involved in that process. Nor was I involved in its aftermath, as the case had gone beyond my level by then. I do know that it was never solved.

Chapter Ten

THE SAD SAGA OF SUZI

esides serving as Humane Investigator for the Bennington County Humane Society, I was also an active volunteer there. In fact, I had been a volunteer before taking on the investigative work. My particular specialty was dog-walking, for the caged dogs hopefully awaiting new owners and new homes. This was a great opportunity to exercise in the lovely Shaftsbury, Vermont vicinity, while helping not-yet-adopted pets to get fresh air and care along the paths and trails near BCHS.

Dog-walkers signed up with BCHS for regular days of the week and times, and then one or more canines were assigned to each of them, requiring some skill in matching animals to volunteers. We were also allowed to express preferences for which dog or dogs we would like to walk, and how long a time we would be walking. Inclement weather and other natural conditions did not necessarily result in walking cancellations, which depended on the walkers' and animals' needs.

In the past, prior to my recruitment as BCHS Humane Agent, I had regularly walked Tucker, a foxhound who appeared purebred, but, as common with shelter dogs, had no papers. Tucker was quite spirited, meaning many prospective adoptive families considered him unmanageable, as he preferred jumping in all directions to straight walking, on occasion knocking over small children. As Tucker's allowed adoption time ran down, I decided to take responsibility for him, as I had come to love him dearly, despite his unruliness, and had no small children he could knock down.

After Tucker's adoption occurred, my dog-walking became a routine at the BCHS headquarters, focusing on a large brown mixed-breed hound named Suzi. She was a very likeable dog, sharing many of Tucker's qualities, including his high-spiritedness. Due to this trait, and her large size, several previous dog walkers had not been able to handle Suzi comfortably -- but I did not mind a challenge and found some techniques such as a very short leash which helped manage the dog. Suzi and I bonded, and she became my regular walking companion three mornings a week.

One day, when I arrived at BCHS to walk Suzi, a technician calmly told me that she had had to be euthanized. I was truly shocked, because she had not yet approached the end of the allowed adoption period, but the same technician said Suzi had begun "shredding her bedding" which was considered a sign of "kennel distress" and therefore keeping her would have been inhumane.

This situation presented a dilemma: on the one hand, proper procedure might have been followed; but on the other hand, Suzi's euthanization seemed very premature and, indeed, unjustified. As the BCHS investigator, I believed I had a responsibility to investigate internal concerns as well as external cases, so I attempted some tactful inquiries about Suzi's demise, to determine if there was more to the story than what the technician had told me. I discovered that Suzi had been seen as a "problem dog" because of being somewhat unmanageable, causing extra time caring for her. The more I tactfully probed the situation, the more I came to believe that her euthanization was done more for the convenience of BCHS shelter staff than out of necessity, which was improper.

It happened that the BCHS President, the wife of one of Bennington's most prominent doctors, was an acquaintance who had fully supported my candidacy as BCHS humane agent; we had worked on several community volunteer projects together, and had a good working relationship. Therefore, I raised the issue of Suzi by a confidential letter sent to her at home, just to be sure it was not intercepted at BCHS, as the agency did not appear to take criticism well. Because the response was confidential, I will not discuss it here; but I concluded that the Bennington

County Humane Society was not as humane as I had previously thought, leading to my grave distress.

Still, there were very few "no-kill" animal shelters in New England, and it is worth considering the reasons for those euthanization policies. Professional shelter animal care is quite expensive, and shelter budgets are always very tight. Intelligent planning is indeed required to operate such a facility effectively, and judgments must be made as to which animals are likely to be adopted, and which are not. Usually, adoption time is the single most important factor in such judgments, which are also colored by an animal's age, condition, and presentability. Many tough calls occur.

With all those considerations, though, **sometimes euthanization is based more on a shelter staff's convenience than on the merits or demerits of an animal's adoptability.** That was true in the case of Suzi, and is likely true in far too many other cases as well. *Rest in peace, Suzi.*

Chapter Eleven

THE RIFT WITH TIFT

One of the peculiarities of the noble State of Vermont, once a Republic until forced in 1791 to join the fledgling American Union by incursions from Massachusetts to the South and New York to the West, is the ongoing existence of certain elected local law enforcement positions such as that of Constable. Many Vermont towns and cities have such Constables, most of whom are responsible officers, even if relatively untrained and uncertified by higher enforcement bodies.

On the other hand, there are the noted and notorious abusers of their law enforcement powers, which brings us to the legendary constable of Wallingford-Mount Tabor, Vermont: Nelson Tift. This particular constable expanded the powers of his minimal office so that his area along Route Seven became a notorious speed trap under the guise of "enforcement of the law". Nelson Tift also managed to make himself an enemy of my right to go through his area, causing numerous detours in order for me to avoid his brand of punitive speed law enforcement for some years.

My first encounter with the "good constable" occurred prior to my assuming duties of Humane Investigator (and thus a fellow law enforcer) for the Bennington County Humane Society. That encounter occurred before a fire closed the Pownal Community Care Home which I then owned. Several residents had asked me to be named in their Advance Directives as the decider of what care they should receive in the event of a life-threatening emergency, particularly whether or not extraordinary measures should be taken when there was little if any hope of recovery. This was a responsibility I never sought – but some residents had no living relatives who might accept it.

One day in early Spring, during a board meeting as a vice president of the Vermont Health Care Association in Montpelier, about three hours north of Pownal, I received a pager alert from my facility that one resident had gone into congestive heart failure, and a decision needed to be made as to what immediate steps should be taken; since I was named in her Advance Directive, I had to travel home at once, causing me to leave the meeting and head back to Pownal with all due haste. That need caused me to rush through Constable Tift's territory a bit over the speed limit of twenty-five miles per hour, and also caused the good Constable to pull my vehicle over. My effort to explain the urgency of the situation, and even my offer to leave my driver's license there and to return the following day for my traffic ticket, fell on Constable Tift's deaf ears; in fact, he had me sit in my car for over half an hour while he did some arcane things in his cruiser, before handing me a ticket with an inflated speed stated. So, after my resident survived this difficult situation, I decided to appear in Rutland court and plead GUILTY WITH AN EXPLANATION.

Lo and behold, on my appointed court date, upon arriving in Rutland an hour north of Pownal, there was Constable Tift waiting for my case to be heard. We each presented our version of the facts of the matter, with my version including reference to this involving a life-or-death decision. Upon hearing the two versions, the judge frowned at the good Constable and said, "Nelson, why did you refuse to let this man carry out Advance Directive duties and then return the next day?" After a minute of silence, with no response beyond a grimace from Constable Tift, my traffic ticket was reduced from a three-point license violation to a minimum one-point infraction; and the judge then gave the good Constable a strong lecture about his poor judgment in the matter. I felt vindicated, but upon recounting the story to my own attorney, he warned me that *"Nelson Tift never forgives and never forgets – he will be out to get you anytime you are in his territory!"*

Fast forwarding to my period as Humane Investigator, my attorney's words turned out to be true. Luckily, Constable Tift's enforcement area was north of my usual investigative territory -- but on occasion I had reason to go through Wallingford, his base, to attend a training session or some agency meeting. My lime-green Honda del Sol was the only one in that part of Vermont, and on many trips the car was followed by the good Constable as I drove well under the speed limit and waved to him. I felt that I was being harassed for having partially bested him in Rutland court, and therefore sent a letter to the Wallingford Select Board, the governing body of his town, to protest Constable Tift's abuse of his minimal law enforcement authority. Surprisingly, the chair of the Select Board wrote back that they had received numerous complaints against the good Constable due to his tactics, but those tactics did indeed raise revenue for the town through fines; further, Tift was a separately-elected official and the Select Board had no authority over him. I was advised to avoid driving through his territory if I did not wish to encounter Constable Tift.

While that guidance seemed somewhat defeatist to me, it also seemed to be the easiest solution. Still, Route Seven is the major north-south artery in that part of Vermont, and any detour added dozens of additional miles to my occasional travel there. Also, perhaps naively, I did not believe any law enforcer, whether elected or appointed, should be allowed to abuse his authority. So, I decided to go one step further and appeal what I saw as Constable Tift's misconduct through over-zealous law enforcement to the Vermont State Police Board, an agency appointed by the State to review dubious practices by comparable officials. I had little to lose by taking this step.

After filing a fully-documented complaint with this Board and waiting several months for any response, I was invited to a meeting of the Board at State Police Headquarters several hours away from Pownal, where I lived (I made sure not to drive through Constable Tift's territory on the way to the meeting.) As matters turned out, my case got short shrift; I was allowed to present it briefly but there were no questions from the senior officers who constituted the Board. Instead I was merely told that I would receive their decision in due course, which took more months. As you might expect, the Board found nothing to fault in Constable Nelson Tift's overzealous speed law enforcement; my complaint was totally dismissed. I never drove through Wallingford again

Chapter Twelve

SAVED BY THE EAGLE

The Eagle to which the title of this chapter of Animal Tales refers is neither an actual bird nor the American symbol, but rather a vehicle somewhat-popular in the 1980s and early 1990s: the AMC Eagle, produced along with Jeeps by the now-defunct American Motors Corporation, which was absorbed into Chrysler Corporation, at which point the AMC Eagle became history. That did not occur, however, before I acquired an old silver AMC Eagle for my humane duties.

The specific reason I purchased my own AMC Eagle was due to snowy and icy Vermont winters which absolutely required four-wheel-drive vehicles for use on the back roads, as was demanded by my humane investigative job duties. While I had several other cars, including the Honda del Sol mentioned in the previous chapter, none of those had four-wheel-drive. I had tried a couple of Subaru station wagons which did have all-wheel-drive, but those

1980s models tended to rust out; one of them went to my son Martin, and the other went to the Bennington homeless shelter, on whose board I was serving. So, as winter approached that year, I searched for an AMC Eagle, finding one which had spent some years in a farm field before being put back on the road again.

The upside of this particular station wagon was its very low mileage, due to being off-the-road for years. What I did not fully comprehend, however, was that there was a downside to that same upside: underneath the car, and not easily seen, was considerable body decay and rusted parts, undoubtedly the result of exposure to the elements in that field, including rain and snow. While the rust on my former Subaru wagons was easy to spot, the Eagle had much hidden decay which did not even come to the attention of the minimal vehicle inspection required in Vermont.

Still, the car served its purpose well in humane investigations for some years, getting through to cases on the backroads and in the backwoods, without getting stuck in deep snow very often. Nor did it slip-and-slide much on frequent ice, as Southern Vermont road coverings would often melt during the day and then re-freeze at night, turning the road surface into a sheet of glare ice. The car's image was enhanced by large magnetic signs on both its sides stating that it was the BCHS HUMANE INVESTIGATIONS vehicle, making it somewhat well-known throughout the area.

While my AMC Eagle was usually serviced by the Bennington Chrysler-Dodge dealer, Alcaro Motors, for routine work such as oil changes I took it to the local Firestone Tire dealer north of town. One fine Spring day, I was on my way to the Bennington County Humane Society (BCHS) to turn in some case reports when the Eagle suddenly slowed down and failed to respond at all to its gas pedal; the car would not run faster than at an idle, which meant it would not go uphill at all. Luckily, I was not far from that Firestone Tire dealer, and by dint of choosing my route to run continuously downhill, I managed to coast into the repair shop and then ask how soon the mechanic on duty could check my vehicle's problem; I was told it would take about an hour to get to it, so I left the Eagle and walked to a fast-food restaurant to get a cup of coffee and wait.

Upon returning to Firestone an hour later, the mechanic informed me that he had gotten to my Eagle and the only problem he could find was that the spring which worked the throttle control had broken, so that the gas pedal did not do anything. A universal spring was used to replace the defective part, and my car was ready to go at minimal cost. Once more, I headed to BCHS to turn in my case reports, after that one-hour delay due to the Eagle's broken throttle spring.

Upon reaching Shaftsbury and BCHS, I heard some crying as I entered their reception area. A husband and wife were standing at the front desk, holding a medium-sized chunky black mixed-breed dog on a leash and the wife was sobbing. As I listened to the intake staff member tell the couple that their dog could not be accepted by the Bennington County Humane Society because of "its cancerous tumors", I began to wonder at this "instant diagnosis" by a BCHS technician, not a veterinarian, but I held my tongue. Instead of challenging that diagnosis, I identified myself and felt around under the chest of the female dog; sure enough, what appeared to the technician as tumors were actually her enlarged nipples, as she apparently had had puppies not too long ago.

Upon asking the couple who had brought the dog in for adoption, they confirmed that diagnosis, while stating that they had come up from Northern Massachusetts to try to find a humane society which would take their dog, as they were moving to a new apartment which did not allow pets. As an "insider" at BCHS I suspected that the real reason for my own humane society refusing to take this dog, which was named Bodi according to the couple, was that it was not very placeable; the dog was gray around the muzzle, not from age but from natural coloring, and rather ugly, as dogs go, along with continually whining in an annoying manner. I believed that BCHS just did not want to be bothered with this difficult-to-place canine, and the staffer had invented "cancer" as an easier way of turning the dog down for placement, to avoid an argument with its owners.

So, after a quick phone call to my own family, I intervened in the situation, offering to take Bodi with no conditions or qualifications, and to provide any needed medical treatment starting with a full veterinary examination by my own veterinarian to insure that Bodi received any needed care. The dog's owners appeared overjoyed -- but the BCHS staff were somewhat taken aback by my offer. Still, this was not the first case in which I had intervened, which is one reason I already had so many dogs and cats; I had vowed to try to take the "unplaceable ones" when I took the job of BCHS Investigative Agent, and Bodi was just the latest to join the growing "pack". Bodi was turned over to me by her owners; we completed and signed all necessary paperwork; and Bodi jumped eagerly into my newly-repaired-and-running AMC Eagle and went home with me, where she remained for many good years as, indeed, she had never had any form of cancer.

This particular incident caused me to view the Bennington County Humane Society with a bit of skepticism, as my trust in BCHS had been damaged by that quick "cancer" diagnosis, although I never got the staffer who made that diagnosis to admit that it had been faked or worsened. But, at the same time, I often wondered whether Bodi's life was actually saved by the fortuitous timing of that throttle spring breaking on my old AMC

Eagle, delaying my arrival at BCHS sufficiently that I got there just as Bodi was being turned down for placement. Was that strange delay a mere accident, or something more? I still wonder about those events today, but there is no doubt that they saved a small dog's life from unnecessary and unjustified euthanizing: ***a very happy result.***

Chapter Thirteen

NO PEACE WITH PEACOCKS

It was a very-early morning call, from an unrecognized male caller, who opened the conversation by saying, "Hey, animal investigator, listen to this!", followed by brief silence on the phone, and then a blood-curdling cry or scream which caused me to literally drop the phone. Upon picking it up again, I asked the caller, "What on earth is that awful noise?" The caller replied that this was a typical mating cry from one of several caged peacocks (located along with a peahen in a nearby cage) quite near his family home on a residential street in Bennington; he claimed that it was mating season, and the peacocks were courting the peahen with "that god-awful racket."

Meanwhile, I had awakened sufficiently to take out my little investigator's notebook; and I begin to write down the particulars of the matter. The caller, as was often the situation, did not want to be identified, but he did provide the location of the peacocks and some additional details, before concluding: "Is there no peace from peacocks?" That seemed a good question, to which I did not have a good answer, as it was something I had never previously pondered. Now, I had no choice.

It took me a couple of hours to get to Bennington from my home, as I had some other tasks to do before tackling this unique "case du jour", including finding my cassette tape recorder in order to record the "god-awful racket." Then, it took me a few minutes more to find the peacocks' home, as the noise had stopped temporarily by then. Upon arriving at the proper location, as indicated by two large cages behind the house — one with both brightly-plumaged male peacocks and the other with the drab peahen – my presence encouraged renewed squeaks, squawks, and screams.

There was no answer when I knocked upon the back door of the house, directly behind the cages. After recording the sounds emanating from the peacocks, and taking a complete set of photos, I went to the homes of several neighbors in order to interview them for reactions to the situation. In such interviews, I always try hard not to "lead" the person being interviewed, but in this case all those interviewed agreed that the noise level was totally unacceptable, interfering with both sleep and waking activities as well. Several of those interviewed stated that worst of all was not knowing just when the "courting calls" would begin again; several neighbors said that they were "on edge all the time" as a result, and one claimed to now be taking sleeping pills as a result.

My major task at that point was to locate the owner of the peacocks, who was well-known to the neighbors whom I was interviewing; she was a leading hairdresser in Bennington, with her own salon in the downtown district. Upon going to the salon, however, one of her staff told me that the owner "had the day off" — and nobody at the salon seemed to know where she was spending that day. So, I left my professional card with a note for her to please call me as soon as possible, which did not happen. Meanwhile, now that her neighbors had been interviewed, I had begun to receive additional neighbors' complaints about unacceptable noise levels several times each day.

My immediate challenge was to track down the peacocks' presumptive owner, who was trying diligently to be unavailable. This was a challenge for several reasons: the neighbors had told me that she had a couple of teenage children, a boy and a girl, who would come home from school in the midafternoon. The neighbors also told me that these children were usually alone in the house at that time, which presented a problem, for two reasons. First, they were not presumptively the owners of the birds, since they were minors who were underage for such ownership. Second, it was my practice to avoid interviewing minors without a relevant adult, such as a parent, present. There were legal issues involved as to interviewing minors alone: generally, not a good idea.

While I was pondering how to resolve this situation by actually approaching the presumptive owner of the peacocks and peahen, the mother of the two teenagers, I took to visiting her house anytime I was in Bennington, which was almost daily, at different times of day. Rather than taking my Animal Investigator vehicle, the AMC Eagle, I would take another car, as actually I had seven vehicles at that time. Being something of a collector of unusual cars, these included a Chrysler Executive Limo, which had been very useful while I was running my community care home, as it could take six passengers and had room for a travel-model wheelchair if necessary. But since Chrysler Corporation had made fewer than a thousand of these limos, mine was the only one registered in Vermont and therefore easily recognizable. However, I also had two nondescript Subaru cars, a sedan and a wagon, so I would drive by the peacock premises in one.

Sure enough, after a few unproductive drive-by trips, one early evening I saw the house owner's car in the driveway (the Vermont State Police cooperated with license plate information.) Upon ringing the doorbell, the owner herself came to the door, and I could not resist the temptation to say, after introducing myself, "We meet at last!" She appeared totally unsurprised when I stated that there were frequent and ongoing complaints about the racket her peacocks made, especially early each morning; she replied, "Well, they're my birds on my land, so it's my problem, isn't it?" My response was,

"No, it is a neighborhood problem, and a likely violation of the town's noise ordinance." We stared at each other for a few moments; then I told her I was reluctant to have to file a formal complaint with the authorities and seek prosecution for noise violations, if it were possible to reach some other solution. She replied, belligerently, "Like what?" So I then asked if she had any relative or friend who lived out in the country and might take all the birds. Her reply was, "Like who?"

Aside from her grammatical error, her attitude was quite annoying; I was led to wonder how to get through to this woman. So, I came up with a "reparative justice" proposal, as follows; I told her: "Well, I could park my Eagle outside your salon, with a big sign saying that you refused to take the slightest step to avoid your birds waking up your neighbors very early each morning!" She then said, "You wouldn't!" and I replied, "Yes, it's a public street – and I would." She then replied, "I'll call your boss and complain you threatened me!" and I replied further that stating a legal option was never a threat, so she could go right ahead. (Actually, I was not sure how the Bennington County Humane Society shelter manager would react to my approach; I did not always have their support, particularly when it came to reparative justice.) We seemed stymied.

So, I decided to try a totally-different tack; I asked her if she really cared about her peacocks' welfare, and she snapped back, "Of course I do. I've had them for years."

That comment led me to reply that since I also cared about their welfare – as well as that of her neighbors – we ought to be able to reach a reasonable solution, as two reasonable people with similar goals. I then asked her if there was some other reasonable option we might explore.

After a few moments of thought, the peacocks' owner said, "Well, I have a salon customer with a farm and no close neighbors; she might take the birds, and let me visit them whenever I wish. I'll call her now." We had been talking outside her front door, which she closed while she went into the front room to make the call. I waited patiently as the conversation continued for minutes; then the peacocks owner came back to the front door and told me, "OK, she will do it, but I had to cut a deal with her. She wants free hair services for six months to take my birds, and I agreed."

And so it came to pass: the peacocks and peahen were relocated to a nearby farm, which I visited after they were settled there, to be sure that the cages and other accommodations were adequate. The owner of the farm was a widow who was quite hard-of-hearing, so early morning crowing did not annoy her, and there were no nearby neighbors. Anyway, farm folks tend to accept more noise than do city folks; for example, people get used to the mooing of cows, particularly when their calves are first separated from them, an annual event on dairy farms. But then, that is a different Animal Tale from that of my one-and-only peacock case, now marked CLOSED.

Chapter Fourteen

ADEPT COMES TO VERMONT

By the late 1990s, I had handled over four hundred animal abuse, neglect, and cruelty cases for the Bennington County Humane Society, which was by then in the process of changing its name to Second Chance Animal Shelter. Meanwhile, I had become an active emergency management volunteer, first in my home town of Pownal, and then regionally through the area preparedness committee which met in Shaftsbury. Truth to tell, I was also becoming a bit bored by then; many animal cases had a similarity and familiarity which was disheartening, while some others were quite unpleasant. Meanwhile, BCHS (or now SCAC) was becoming a mite bossy, with a new shelter manager who came from higher education with little practical animal experience. My own wings were in danger of being clipped, particularly as to reparative justice solutions, making me somewhat less enthusiastic about my humane investigative work.

Therefore, when I received an impressive letter of invitation from then-Governor of Vermont Dr. Howard Dean, whom I had met on several occasions in our small State, I jumped at the chance to join a vital new group which had been assigned the task of planning for the handling of domestic animals in emergencies and crises, both in their own local areas and Statewide. Since this was a volunteer position appointment, my own shelter agreed to cover some travel expenses to monthly meetings in Montpelier, the State capitol, about three hours away from my home by car. These meetings were chaired by the State Veterinarian or another Vermont state official involved with animal matters. Since Montpelier is rather cosmopolitan (for Vermont, at least), I always arrived early, having a good Oriental lunch and looking around the stores before going to the meeting. One of the best things about volunteer groups is that your time is your own, up to the meeting.

Our first substantive issue was choosing a less-awkward name than the one used to convene our first meeting. Indeed, there had been no real name at all; the invitation merely stated that each invitee had some special role regarding animal welfare in Vermont, and had been invited to join a new "task force" to help develop a State plan for promoting animal welfare in disasters and emergencies. Turning that complex concept into a short-and-catchy group title was challenging.

As I thought about this naming challenge, I recalled that many years earlier I had been involved with a sports car rally club based in New London, Connecticut; that newly-established club was seeking a catchy name, and I came up with **Southeastern Connecticut Auto-sports Team**: **SCAT** for short. That name was enthusiastically accepted by our group, and was probably the highlight of my leadership; I never won any rallies, and my Volvo P1800 two-seater eventually rusted out.

Still, as I tried to think up a good acronym for this fledgling Vermont animal-protection group, what suddenly popped into my mind was: **Animals in Disasters Emergency Planning Team, or ADEPT** for short. Upon proposing that title, and since nobody had a better idea, it was accepted: **ADEPT** we were. For the next several years, we went about vital Statewide planning for animal care in disasters. Eventually, our final plan was accepted as official Vermont animal guidance.

As to why such official State animals-in-disasters guidance is needed: that is a rather complex issue, and an important one, since other States have not necessarily provided such protections. To understand some of the factors and implications for companion animals during emergencies and disasters, one must understand that **relief agencies such as the Red Cross offer assistance to disaster victims, including emergency housing – but not to their dogs and cats! *When it comes to companion animals, there is indeed "no room at the inn" – or at any other facility.***

Case in point: the policies applied by the American Red Cross emergency managers in my own area, where facilities such as schools and fire stations were made available to those evacuated in a disaster, but only providing that they were willing to leave their companion animals behind. A typical experience, for example, was the frequent flooding of the Alta Gardens Trailer Park near me, which was situated on low and swampy land near the base of the local semi-mountain. At the time of Spring water runoff each year, Alta Gardens tended to turn from a swamp to a small lake, endangering trailers, RVs, and residents therein by exposing them to likely electrical risks. As the town's volunteer emergency management coordinator, I was tasked to assist evacuations of the human occupants of Alta Gardens – **as long as they left their dogs, cats, and other pets behind!** Many pet owners were totally unwilling to do so, preferring to "go down with the ship", even risking potential electrocution as waters rose and wires under trailers sparked or shorted out. **ADEPT's worthy goals included plans to avoid or reduce such risky situations.**

Fast forwarding to the present, such tragic disasters as major hurricanes along the Gulf of Mexico coast, frequent tornados in the Midwest and beyond, and seemingly-endless forest fires in the Western United States, are causing ever-increasing risks to the welfare, well-being, and very lives of companion, farm, and wild animals in growing areas of North America. While strong efforts are made to protect and save human lives, little attention is given to such life-or-death situations for animals living in these endangered areas. It may seem ironic that the news media love to cover stories of occasional "reunions" of companion animals with their families, but far less media attention is devoted to more-frequent losses of all types of animals in disasters. **Residents of high-risk areas should learn how to handle those disaster risks to all types of animals well in advance of need.** *Each of us has a role to play in saving animals in disasters.*

Chapter Fifteen

ACO ON THE GO!

With this chapter, as with my life, a new direction had emerged. In order to understand how that major change occurred, a bit of background is needed. After four years as humane investigator for the Bennington County Human Society (BCHS) in Southern Vermont, I accepted the position of hazard mitigation consultant to the New Hampshire Office of Emergency Management, based in Concord on the campus of the former State Hospital. Having served as volunteer emergency management coordinator for my then-home town of Pownal, Vermont, I had developed a deep interest in the optimal handling of both natural and societal disasters (the latter type including terrorism.) That interest led to my training by FEMA (the Federal Emergency Management Agency) at their facility near Boston, leading to my receiving postings of relevant open jobs..

As the millennial year 2000 approached, I had handled over four hundred animal abuse, neglect, and cruelty cases in Bennington County, Vermont, with consultations and assistance on cases elsewhere in the Southern portion of the State. Meanwhile, the work of the ADEPT team was wrapping up, as we prepared our final version of the State plan to handle companion and farm animals in disasters for submission to Gov. Howard Dean and the State Legislature. I began to feel that, while there was no end to animal problems, issues, and needs, my own work was done.

Therefore, when I received a posting for two emergency management positions available at the official New Hampshire State agency, it seemed very natural to apply on at least one of those openings. Ironically, however, the position on which I decided to apply was not the one which I was actually offered. Shortly after being interviewed for that first open position, I received a call from the New Hampshire State Hazard Mitigation Officer (or SHMO, an amusing acronym) who told me that I had not been chosen for the position for which I had been interviewed – rather, he was offering me the other position, for which I had not applied as it called for the credential of Professional Engineer, which I did not possess. So I asked the SHMO why it was being offered to me when I lacked that necessary credential, and he replied: *'Well, we did not get a single Professional Engineer to apply, so it seems you are the best we can do."* I accepted at once.

My official title would be Hazard Mitigation Consultant, and my basic job duty was to secure completion of over forty projects funded with Hurricane Floyd emergency funds which had been granted several years before, in order to mitigate or reduce a variety of risks to New Hampshire cities and towns. It seemed that more than three dozen of those projects had not been completed. My job was to get them finished within the next fifteen months, by the end of March 2002, when those remaining grant funds would be exhausted. There was a lot of heel-dragging on the part of some municipalities, so it was my newly-accepted job to get those projects done by the deadline.

The first challenge, though, was to relocate to the Concord, New Hampshire area from Southern Vermont. Luckily, there was a solution: my Southwind RV was available, and after checking the options near Concord, I decided to move the vehicle from Vermont to an RV park in Epsom, a half-hour East of Concord, along with my two favorite dogs, Tucker the foxhound and Domino the Rottmatian (half Rottweiler, half Dalmatian.) My other animals would remain in Vermont, with a local caregiver in charge. This move was accomplished at the start of 2001, allowing me to undertake the new Hazard Mitigation position as soon as it was available, and I was able to get all but two of the outstanding projects completed by March of 2002, when its grant funds ran out.

By then, other changes in my life caused me to give up the Southwind RV in favor of a cottage on Emerald Lake in Hillsborough, NH, a half hour east of Concord, which became my weekend retreat. Meanwhile, during weekdays, I had returned to the field of working with animals – but in a new capacity, as I had been appointed Animal Control Officer for the Town of Farmington, New Hampshire, relocating to half of a duplex house along the major highway serving the Town.

My background as humane investigator for the Bennington County Humane Society, combined with the end of grant funding for my hazard mitigation work for the New Hampshire Office of Emergency Management, led to my applying for the open ACO post with the Farmington Police Department. My required training for humane investigators frequently involved animal control officers as well, and I had worked closely with all of them in Bennington County, Vermont; there was partnership and mutual respect among all those responsible for animal concerns in our area, although the emphasis differed somewhat, with ACOs focusing heavily on residents' welfare too.

In the interest of full disclosure, I must add that some of my previous experiences with ACOs in both Vermont and New Hampshire were not very satisfactory. Case in point: my dog Domino was viciously attacked by a neighbor's dog in Hillsborough while we walked to the mailboxes, and was bitten painfully as a result. Repeated calls to the Hillsborough ACO only reached his message tape;

and he never responded to the need to protect not only animals, but also residents, from being mauled and bitten by this same nasty dog. That type of experience helped motivate me to become Farmington's ACO, knowing that I would take the job seriously and focus on the welfare of both the Town's human and animal residents. I was enthusiastically sworn in as ACO.

It did not take long to discover that ACO duties were quite different from those of any humane investigator. Some of those new duties were rather routine, such as conducting "rabies clinics" in which local dogs and cats were vaccinated against that dread disease, usually at reduced cost. Other activities ranged from investigating animal concerns which were annoying local residents, including frequently-barking or occasionally-biting dogs, and defecations found on local lawns. Many such cases turned out to be pretexts for other long-simmering neighborhood or town issues with the alleged animal concerns substituted for those other matters. I found that hand-holding was often needed in such cases, as soothing the hurt feelings of some complainants was enough to resolve the complaint; the local resident just wanted reassurance that some town official cared!

Other cases, though, were far more serious. It was not unusual for people arrested for "driving under the influence" to be driving with their dog in the car or truck; then, I would be called to retrieve the animal and take it to the local holding pens, located on the premises of the landfill. Often such calls came in late-at-night, resulting in some sleepless nights; also often, animals in such vehicles did not want to be removed by an ACO, particularly after the arresting officer had tried and failed to get the animal to vacate. It did not take long for me to discover that saying "nice doggy" while pulling on a rope around the animal's forequarters was not a safe practice.

Still, I had the consolation that at least my orientation had the animal's best interest at heart -- which is not always the case with Animal Control Officers, most of whom come from a police background rather than having once been humane investigators. In the Town of Farmington, however, the ACO position was only half-time, and even as an adjunct police officer, I was given considerable leeway in the performance of my duties. After initial training, neither the police chief, nor the lieutenant to whom I reported, was likely to interfere with my duties. I was therefore allowed to put animals first, insofar as possible; when there was adverse feedback from animal owners or local residents, it was usually shrugged off by departmental and town officials.

A few months after my initial training, followed by carrying out actual ACO duties, I heard that a nearby town, Bradford, New Hampshire, was also seeking a part-time Animal Control Officer. In addition to duties for the Town of Farmington, I was then teaching business and economics courses as adjunct faculty at Plymouth State University in Plymouth, New Hampshire. So, at first, I was reluctant to apply for the Bradford ACO opening; but upon reviewing its parameters, I found that duties there were on a case-by-case basis, without any minimal time requirement. That fact led me to apply, and the Town of Bradford Select Board appointed me as Town ACO.

Serving as ACO for two different Town Police Departments, some twenty miles apart, plus teaching at Plymouth State University, kept me very busy. I found that I was on-call for animal cases and issues around the clock, and more than once had to rescue a dog or cat from a wrecked vehicle, or after a driver had been arrested for drunk or drugged driving, often very late at night -then, the next morning, driving over an hour to Plymouth for an early-morning economics class. This turned out to be quite a stressful routine, made even more stressful by issues within the Town of Bradford which were clearly affecting its Police Department – and ultimately its ACO.

Whereas Farmington had a happy police department, with excellent leadership and popular cops, Bradford was going through some kind of Town soul-searching which turned out to include its police. Being only a part-time ACO and not a Town of Bradford resident, I knew few details of the issues involved, and had no "inside knowledge" at all. Still, my wife and I did socialize with the department, including holiday parties and other occasions, and there were undercurrents of concern as to the future of the departmental leadership – especially the police chief's future. He had had a falling out with some of the Town Select Board, and it turned out that his days as Chief were numbered. While this had no direct impact on the ACO position, I had decided to resign if the Chief was wrongfully terminated. When that occurred, though, I procrastinated for months, hoping the Chief's replacement would also be both competent and caring about animal welfare.

In that hope, though, I was immensely disappointed, as the Bradford Select Board decided to just have the Police Chief in nearby New London, New Hampshire take over the vacant Bradford position on a temporary basis. The way in which I learned of that decision was via a call from that acting Police Chief, telling me to meet with him the next day to "discuss the ACO position." When that meeting occurred, I was told that it had been decided to "contract out the ACO's duties" and my services were therefore no longer needed. Although I was disappointed at the time, this actually turned out to be a blessing, as ACO cases in Bradford always seemed to be difficult at best, and impossible in some instances.

Consider, for example, the case of a local Bradford family which was running a "petting zoo farm" which allowed children to encounter farm animals after paying a modest entry admission. Several visitors to that farm had complained of deplorable conditions for the cows, sheep, and other animals on display, including old feces and uneaten food being left inside their facilities. Upon visiting that family farm, I found the reports to be accurate, and gave the owners a couple of weeks to "clean up their act" and their farm. The result, however, was several local letters published in the Bradford weekly newspaper which complained that the farm's owners were being "picked on" or "singled out" for overzealous animal control law enforcement. Once Town sympathies appeared to be on the side of the petting zoo's ownership, I was told to back off on my enforcement efforts, or as one Town official put it: "Just leave them in peace." Given this total lack of back-up by Town of Bradford authorities, I was just as happy to stop being ACO.

None of that, however, affected my duties as Farmington's ACO, which remained half-time there until more than a year had passed. Then, the Town Manager notified me that there were several other vacant part-time official Farmington positions available, should I wish to be considered for them. That news left me with a bit of a dilemma, as I was also teaching half-time at Plymouth State University, recently upgraded from the former Plymouth State College as more majors were added. One did not have to be a mathematician to know that two Farmington half-time jobs plus a half-time teaching job added up to more than full-time work; on the other hand, since the Farmington jobs were pretty-much "on call", it might be worth a try at doing all of them. Thus, in addition to being the Town ACO, I also became its Deputy Health Officer and Code Enforcer. (However, those additional jobs usually did not involve animals, so are not covered herein.)

Returning to describing work as Farmington's Animal Control Officer: I became an active sworn police officer for the first time in my life, finding a great deal of camaraderie present within the ranks of this "happy police department." I had wondered if I would be treated as an integral part of the department, or as just a hanger-on or pseudo-cop; the former turned out to be true, so after spending time most days writing up my reports at the police station, I socialized with as fine a set of officers as ever existed in New Hampshire. What I discovered was that, not only were they dedicated to enforcing a complex set of State and local laws, including some rather weird ones – they were also very dedicated to each other. While the police chief and his lieutenant assistant were relatively mature, most of the officers were recent graduates of police training programs.

I found out about that camaraderie early in my tenure as Town ACO, when I happened to mention the deplorable condition of the animal cages which the Town kept near the local landfill. These were essentially holding pens for lost or stray animals, and also for animals removed from their owners for some violation of law, or at least of proper animal care practices. Occasionally, for example, some hunting dog owners would follow an abysmal practice to "toughen" hounds or beagles by leaving them chained up outside, in all sorts of weather, including sub-zero temps and even during snow or ice storms. In such cases, if an owner refused to take his dogs inside his home or trailer, Animal Control would issue a citation; and then transport the dogs to the Town holding pens temporarily, while seeking a court order to confiscate the animals and take them to a local animal shelter. Since the owner would have to pay boarding costs there, usually things did not go that far; upon a promise to follow the law and keep the dogs inside during severe weather, they would be released to the owner, who would meet me at the holding pens to retrieve them. Often, there would be comments about conditions at those pens being worse than at home.

One early Spring day, I was writing up a case report related to these holding cages, and happened to comment that they were in deplorable condition, dirty and rusty, and sometimes insecure due to poor-fitting or rusty wire sides and old locks. One of our officers, Aaron, volunteered to take the next weekend to "fix up the cages." I gratefully accepted his offer; that Saturday, Aaron came to the Town landfill with a whole work crew, tools, materials, and enthusiasm; by afternoon, the cages had been repaired -- and even replaced in a couple of cases, via a local hardware store. It was great to find that my fellow officers cared enough to give up a weekend day to help animals.

Another occasion for Farmington Police Department solidarity was the annual Rabies Clinic, during which local companion animals were vaccinated against that dread disease at minimal cost. As Animal Control Officer, I was responsible for all aspects of the Rabies Clinic, from recruiting animal owners to bring their pets and publicizing the event to insuring sufficient staff to carry out the vaccinations. There were some touchy aspects, such as would occur when an unlicensed dog was brought in for vaccination; technically, its owner should have received a citation for not having licensed the animal; but that always seemed like a form of entrapment, so I usually just told the owner to get the license within the next week, and then followed up as needed. In such cases, owners often used the Rabies Clinic as an opportunity for licensing.

Less enjoyable, though, were the occasional serious cases which occurred in Farmington and Bradford. One of these involved a fox behaving strangely, by challenging pedestrians and even motorists on a town back road; normally, wildlife was not my responsibility, but this fox had many symptoms of being rabid, and that situation fell within my jurisdiction. Upon going to the site and finding the animal standing in the middle of the road with its teeth bared while foaming at the mouth, I called for a regular police officer to come and do what was needed to shoot the fox. Upon being tested, it did prove to be rabid, resulting in my having to publicize that fact in the local weekly newspaper and request reports of any similar situations or cases. Luckily, the rabid fox was an isolated incident, and thus the only rabies case which I had to handle. Amen.

Chapter Sixteen

WOLFGANG THE WILD

n order to end ***Animal Tales*** on a high note, it concludes with the story of Wolfgang the Wild, a wolf-dog hybrid whose type was occasionally found in Northern New England. There were still wolves living in dens in the "outback", a fact not always noted in regional descriptions; and on occasion they would breed with German Shepherds and other large dogs. This is the true tale of one such wolf-dog hybrid, which my wife and I named Wolfgang the Wild, as it became part of our extended "animal family."

While I was still serving as Town of Farmington Animal Control Officer, we had moved from Farmington to Gonic, New Hampshire, a suburb of Rochester adjacent to Farmington, after our landlady (whom we called The Troll privately) demanded a massive rent increase. We had saved our mutual duplex home from burning down when The Troll left the stove on and then left the house;

following which we smelled smoke coming from her side of the duplex and called the fire department, which extinguished the spreading blaze. The Troll's way of showing appreciation was to nearly double our rent after our lease expired; we always suspected that perhaps the stove fire was not accidental and we were being punished for saving our mutual home, but that was merely unprovable suspicion. On the other hand, we refused to pay that massive rent increase; nor did we feel totally safe living there, in case our suspicions were correct. We managed to find a separate house on a quiet street in Gonic, with the additional advantage of being within easy walking distance of an impressive waterfall along the local river. We jumped at the chance to relocate and leave the Troll, moving to Gonic as soon as our lease had expired. Since the Town of Bradford had contracted out Animal Control, only my duties in Farmington remained.

One bright Winter day, I received a call from the Farmington Police Department that a local resident wanted to give up his dog and it would need to be transported to an Animal Shelter. There were several shelters with which we worked, which took in our strays and unwanted companion animals for a fee (we tried to get previous owners to pay that fee, but often failed). My usual procedure was to first pick up the dog or cat usually involved (occasionally exotic animals were being given up, but often snakes or birds could be sold by their owners) and place it in one of the Farmington holding cages while a shelter placement was arranged; that way, if the animal needed immediate veterinary care or other service, it could be handled locally. My private reason for this extra step was to help insure that shelters would not quickly euthanize a "problem animal" which appeared scruffy, distressed, or whose care might be costly to a shelter. The nearest and only New Hampshire "no kill" shelter was several hours away from Farmington; and often there was "no room at the inn" for problem-animals from beyond that shelter's area.

On this particular call, I immediately noticed that the animal I was asked to retrieve was different from most of my pick-ups, having a longer coat of gray-brown fur than was typical for a large-size dog. The animal's presumptive owner, who came to the door of his run-down home, was somewhat different also, being more unkempt and scruffy than his animal. He told me he had been given the animal by an unidentified friend, but could no longer afford to feed it as "it eats like a horse." So, upon the owner's signing the necessary surrender form, I took the animal.

By then, it was getting dark, as New England winter days are quite short, and I was getting tired, so I decided to take the animal home overnight and place it in a holding cage the following day. While it was the size of a German Shepherd, it appeared quite docile and friendly; part of my motivation in bringing it home was my wife's penchant for German Shepherds, her favorite breed. That night, though, we discovered one bad habit of the animal, when our sleep was disrupted by a sound somewhat like

Niagara Falls: it was not trained to do its business outside, as we had taken it for a walk before bedtime, but it seemed to prefer our family room for its toilet.

The following morning, before taking the animal to a holding cage in Farmington, my wife and I took it for a walk, hoping to avoid another Niagara Falls in our family room; along the way, we met a boy about ten years old who asked whether our newfound animal was a wolf; that thought had not really crossed our minds, so I told the lad that it was "part German Shepherd." He replied that it looked very much like a wolf to him, and went on his way; I began to ponder his words, leading to some internet research upon returning home. Indeed, upon checking on the computer, our new animal appeared to be a member of the grey wolf species, having most of that species distinguishing characteristics. That likelihood had not occurred to me when I took the animal.

Under the circumstances, my wife and I were in a very difficult situation, as fully-male wolves were not allowed in New Hampshire; the animal would need to be either neutered or euthanized at once, and no local animal shelter would be willing to take any responsibility for a part-wolf! We decided to procrastinate by holding onto our new friend, at least temporarily, starting with giving him a name; the logical choice was Wolfgang, composer Mozart's middle name. Thus, Wolfgang the Wild became part of our animal household, being on good terms with

Domino, our only dog at that time. When I submitted the paperwork on Wolfgang to the Farmington Police Department, I conveniently omitted any references to his wolf lineage.

Nevertheless, we realized we could not keep Wolfgang the Wild permanently; being an Animal Control Officer, I was required to take New Hampshire's relevant laws seriously, and my wife and I were indeed breaking the law banning male unneutered wolf hybrids from residence there. Further, living in a small rented house in Gonic, with an animal which was not cooperative as to training to do its business outside the premises, we would soon have "landlord problems" there. We had to find another placement for Wolfgang the Wild, the sooner the better – and safer, too; while Wolfgang had a very sweet disposition, we did notice some resistance on occasion, which might turn more forceful if put to the test. That was a chance we were not prepared to take.

Further internet research on these issues led to our discovery of a refuge for wolf-dog hybrids, in the wild country right along the Northern New Hampshire-Vermont border, in a mountain area pretty much ignored by law enforcers in both states. Purposely avoiding being too specific, I will just indicate that some seventy animals were kept there at the time, through the loving care of a rather-wolfish looking man and several of his minions, all of them dedicated to saving these unwanted animals in the wild environment, or as close to that as could be achieved at present.

Upon calling that wolf refuge, via a phone number found on the internet, and describing our situation regarding Wolfgang the Wild, the refuge proprietor agreed to have us bring Wolfgang there the following Saturday; he did not commit to taking the animal off our hands, but since we had no better option, we decided to make the four-hour-each-way trip North to the refuge. We started out on Interstate 93, walking Wolfgang several times at rest areas along the way, and then exiting onto highways and secondary roads via map directions the "wolfmaster," as we termed the refuge proprietor, had provided over the phone. Nearing his territory, the terrain became wild and the roads were in very poor shape, full of potholes and rather muddy, and a challenge even for our Blazer vehicle. After an hour of difficult "white knuckle" travel, we finally arrived.

The headquarters for the wolf preserve was a rather-large wooden one-story building with some parking out in front; the proprietor came outside when we pulled in, and we escorted Wolfgang from the Blazer to be inspected. After checking him over quite thoroughly, "from stem to stern" as the saying goes, the proprietor pronounced Wolfgang about seventy percent true Eastern wolf, and thus eligible for refuge there. We had already passed some large cages as we entered, and had also noted numerous "wolfish-looking" animals roaming around the premises.

Without further ado, Wolfgang was escorted to a large holding pen and placed inside, with a bone to gnaw. The proprietor told us that he would be checked by an unidentified "friendly" veterinarian on Monday, and then gradually released to wander at large with most of the other part-wolves on the premises. We were offered the opportunity to make a donation, and did so quite willingly. Then we bid a fond farewell to Wolfgang, staying in touch with the preserve for some time afterwards, and learning that he had adapted to living in the wild with other part-wolves, and was doing well there. We missed Wolfgang the Wild, but not so much his nightly Niagara Falls.

Here, with the true story of Wolfgang, ends the body of **Animal Tales**. My work as an Animal Control Officer in Farmington, New Hampshire continued until we moved South to Georgia in 2008, to be nearer family there. We relocated to Dahlonega, Georgia, a charming small city in the North Georgia foothills, and I investigated taking on Animal Control work again – finding that this was done by full-time officers of the local Sheriff's Department, and was not for me. Teaching at area colleges and trying to adjust to the Southland were sufficient challenges, in any event. Still, I have missed professional work as Humane Investigator and ACO; hence, this book.

AFTERWORD

We humans share our only planet, the Earth, with a host of other species of both animals and plants – even if the number of that host is diminishing, due primarily to environmental issues caused largely by human actions, and inaction. It is therefore our absolute moral imperative to behave as "good shepherds" of the Earth and of all of its present species. Lately, we have been ignoring or refusing that moral and mortal responsibility, at our peril, as we degrade the planet; and eliminate or drastically reduce so many forms of life. The crises in the Amazon Basin and our remaining coral reefs are clear signs of these trends, and of the drastic need for restoration.

Animal Tales is based in part upon these premises. Both as a Humane Investigator and as an Animal Control Officer, its author often had to make difficult choices and decisions, as to which cases required speedy and sometimes drastic actions, and then exactly what actions were needed. As pointed out in the chapter on reparative justice, and elsewhere, *Animal Tales* contends that often all of the established options and choices were poor, or at least inadequate to resolve the problems at hand. On occasion, then, its author went beyond the established law and practices.

It is indeed a "slippery slope" to use reparative justice and other novel techniques in trying to resolve some animal problems and situations. It can also be essential to do so, for the reality is that established animal laws are inadequate and insufficient to handle many situations; and such issues are further compounded by the lukewarm-or-less enforcement of such laws. Those basic contentions are illustrated by the cases covered throughout *Animal Tales*, as well as by dozens of additional cases handled by its author. Those basic contentions also led to some of the rules and regulations which became part of the work of **ADEPT**, the Animals in Disasters Emergency Planning Team in Vermont, on which this author served actively and proactively for years.

There is nothing sacred about the present set of statutes, laws, rules, regulations, and practices followed in both humane investigation and animal control. Indeed, the inadequacy of those laws and customs should be clear, not only to professionals in the field, but to concerned citizens as well. If some reparative justice and other similar techniques discussed herein go a bit further, it is in a good cause, and often with good results. Sometimes, the road leading down the slippery slope needs to be taken, as in some of the cases described in **Animal Tales.** We owe at least that much to the many creatures with whom we share Planet Earth. Indeed, we owe them much more!

Eugene F. Elander, Long Beach, California, and Gotland, Sweden Autumn, SPRING 2021

AUTHOR BIO

D r. Eugene Elander won the Young Poets Award at 16 from the Dayton, Ohio Poets Guild for his poem The Vision. He was chosen Poet Laureate of Pownal, Vermont for his poem Pownal People, and was a leading contender for the post of Poet Laureate of Rochester, New Hampshire. His three new verses titled America the Beautiful: September 11, 2001, memorializing the terrorist tragedy, have been widely acclaimed and were read into the Congressional Record by then- Connecticut U.S. Senator Chris Dodd. Dr. Elander has authored four volumes of poetry: The Right Click, The World Click, Journeyings, and Philosophy over Fika (two of which were co-authored with his wife Birgit) -- as well as two published novels: The Goat of God, and Turning the Tides, available via Signalman Press. A self-help book titled Empowerment: Taking Charge of your Life has just been completed and published via Amazon KDP (Kindle Direct Publishing). In Summer, 2018, Dr. Elander completed his magnum opus, My Many Miracles: A Spiritual Journey, recently published by Lang Book Publishing.. Dr. Elander is a freelance columnist who published a newspaper for ten years in New London, CT. He is an economist and col-lege lecturer, and has been an agency executive director, emergency management consultant, investigator; and former animal control officer, deputy code enforcement and health officer for Farmington, New Hampshire. He continues to both teach and tutor on-ground and on-line economics and business courses

He and his wife Birgit divide their time between Southern California, USA, and her homeland, Gotland, Sweden. They have also traveled extensively through-out North America and Europe. The Elanders have children and grandchildren whom they visit regularly in Minneapolis, the Los Angeles area; and in Gotland. Several other books by Dr. Elander are underway, includ-ing a public version of his doctoral thesis on Cooperatism, a new economic system he designed which includes all stakeholders (workers, consumers, and the public as well as stockholders) in crucial decision making. Dr. Elander is an original member of the Stonepile Writers group in North Georgia, affiliated with the University of North Georgia, which has anthologized a number of his poems; and a former member of the Poetry Society of New Hampshire. He is an Op-Ed contributor to various progressive causes, news media & websites, and is President of his own firms Elander Press and Elander Enterprises.

The inspiration for Animal Tales came from Dr. Elander's parents: his beloved mother Anne, who first rescued cats and dogs for many years in person, and later via a host of contributions to worthy animal causes all over North America; and his father Martin, who rescued Rusty and Springer, both discussed at the start of Animal Tales. May they also frolic forever in the Pastures of Plenty with all the Elander animal friends!